My Collection of

This folder will allow you to keep your four best texts along with relevant drafts safely in one place. From these, you will choose the two final texts for your **Classroom-Based Assessment** and write them out again in the space provided at the back of the folder.

The folder contains:

- A **sample contents page** with a list of four texts in different genres. This sample includes an illustration and a dedication.

- A **contents template** on which you can list your four texts in different genres, your name and date of publication. Add an illustration and a dedication if you wish.

- Pages to write final versions of each of your **four texts** (or you can type and insert them).

- A **Reflection Sheet** is provided after each text to give you practice in filling them out.

- Pages and Reflection Sheets for your **final two chosen texts**.

- A pocket at the back to include **earlier drafts** of your work.

A note on genres (different types of texts)

In the sample contents, the four genres are a short story, a radio play, a speech and a television news broadcast. There are many other genres that you could choose: letter, debate, dialogue, chapter from a memoir, news broadcast, scene from a play or film, newspaper editorial, article, advertisement, sports article, etc.

MY COLLECTION OF TEXTS 1

Contents

Title of text	Genre	Page
1. *The Glass Palace*	Short story	x
Reflection Note		x
2. *Journey into the Unknown*	Radio play	x
Reflection Note		x
3. 'Children of the 21st century'	Speech	x
Reflection Note		x
4. 'Ireland Triumphs!'	Sports article	x
Reflection Note		x
Final Text 1 *The Glass Palace*	Short story	x
Reflection Note		x
Final Text 2 'Ireland Triumphs!'	Sports article	x
Reflection Note		x

Author Luke K. Steinbeck
(*many authors include their middle names or initials*)

Date of publication November 2016

This collection is dedicated to my grandmother, who read to me before I could read myself.

Ireland Triumphs!

2 FIRE AND ICE 2

My Contents

	Title of text	Genre	Page
1.	_____	_____	
	_____		4
	Reflection Note		8
2.	_____	_____	
	_____		9
	Reflection Note		13
3.	_____	_____	
	_____		14
	Reflection Note		18
4.	_____	_____	
	_____		19
	Reflection Note		22

Final Text 1 _____

_____ 23

Reflection Note 27

Final Text 2 _____

_____ 28

Reflection Note 32

Author _____

Date of
publication _____

This collection is dedicated to

_____

_____

_____

Caption:

Background courtesy of Freepik

Text 1 Title: _____

_____

Genre: _____

MY COLLECTION OF TEXTS

MY COLLECTION OF TEXTS

The Collection of the Student's Texts
STUDENT REFLECTION NOTE

SCHOOL	STUDENT

TITLE and GENRE

I chose this genre because ...

My assessment of my work ...

What I learned from creating this text	What I would do differently next time

Student	Teacher	Date

Text 2 Title: _____

_____

Genre: _____

MY COLLECTION OF TEXTS

FIRE AND ICE 2

MY COLLECTION OF TEXTS

FIRE AND ICE 2

The Collection of the Student's Texts
STUDENT REFLECTION NOTE

SCHOOL	STUDENT

TITLE and GENRE

I chose this genre because ...

My assessment of my work ...

What I learned from creating this text	What I would do differently next time

Student	Teacher	Date

Text 3 Title: _____

_____

Genre: _____

MY COLLECTION OF TEXTS

MY COLLECTION OF TEXTS

The Collection of the Student's Texts
STUDENT REFLECTION NOTE

SCHOOL	STUDENT

TITLE and GENRE

I chose this genre because ...

My assessment of my work ...

What I learned from creating this text	What I would do differently next time

Student	Teacher	Date

Text 4 Title: _____

_____

Genre: _____

MY COLLECTION OF TEXTS

FIRE AND ICE 2

MY COLLECTION OF TEXTS

The Collection of the Student's Texts
STUDENT REFLECTION NOTE

SCHOOL

STUDENT

TITLE and GENRE

I chose this genre because ...

My assessment of my work ...

What I learned from creating this text

What I would do differently next time

Student

Teacher

Date

Final Text 1: _____

_____

Genre: _____

MY COLLECTION OF TEXTS

The Collection of the Student's Texts
STUDENT REFLECTION NOTE

SCHOOL

STUDENT

TITLE and GENRE

I chose this genre because ...

My assessment of my work ...

What I learned from creating this text

What I would do differently next time

Student

Teacher

Date

Final Text 2: _____

_____

Genre: _____

MY COLLECTION OF TEXTS

FIRE AND ICE 2

MY COLLECTION OF TEXTS

The Collection of the Student's Texts
STUDENT REFLECTION NOTE

SCHOOL	STUDENT

TITLE and GENRE

I chose this genre because ...

My assessment of my work ...

What I learned from creating this text	What I would do differently next time

Student	Teacher	Date